BRAIN GAMING for Clever Kids

Puzzles and solutions
by Dr. Gareth Moore
B.Sc (Hons), M.Phil, Ph.D.

Illustrations and cover
artwork by Chris Dickason

Designed by Janene Spencer
and Zoe Bradley

Edited by Imogen Williams

Cover Design by Angie Allison

BRAIN GAMING for Clever Kids

BARRON'S

First edition for the United States and Canada published
in 2018 by Barron's Educational Series, Inc.

First published in Great Britain in 2018 by
Buster Books, an imprint of Michael O'Mara
Books Limited, 9 Lion Yard,
Tremadoc Road, London SW4 7NQ

Puzzles and solutions © 2018 Gareth Moore
Illustrations and layouts © 2018 Buster Books

All inquiries should be addressed to:
Barron's Educational Series, Inc.
250 Wireless Boulevard
Hauppauge, New York 11788
www.barronseduc.com

Library of Congress Control Number: 2018940832
ISBN: 978-1-4380-1237-7

Date of Manufacture: May 2018
Manufactured by: M19A19R, Louisville (Quebec), Canada

Printed in Canada
9 8 7 6 5 4 3 2 1

INTRODUCTION

Are you ready for a brain-busting challenge? This book contains over 100 Brain Gaming puzzles, which are designed to test every part of your brain. Each Brain Game can be tackled on its own, but the puzzles get steadily harder as the book progresses, so you might want to start at the front and work your way through.

At the top of every page there is a space for you to write how much time it took you to complete each game. Don't be afraid to make notes on the pages—this can be a good tactic to help you keep track of your thoughts as you work on a puzzle. There are some blank pages at the back of the book that you can use for figuring out your answers.

Read the simple instructions on each page before tackling a puzzle. If you get stuck, read the instructions again in case there's something you missed. Work in pencil so you can erase things and try again if you need to.

If you are still stuck, you could also try asking an adult, although did you know that your brain is actually much more powerful than a grown-up's? When you get older, your brain will get rid of lots of information it thinks it doesn't need any more, which means you might be better at solving these games than older people are.

If you're **REALLY** stuck, have a peek at the answers at the back of the book, and then try and figure out how you could have arrived at that solution yourself.

Now, good luck and have fun!

Introducing the Brain Games Master:
Gareth Moore, B.Sc (Hons), M.Phil, Ph.D.

Dr. Gareth Moore is an Ace Puzzler, and author of lots of puzzle and brain-training books.

He created an online brain-training site called BrainedUp.com, and runs an online puzzle site called PuzzleMix.com. Gareth has a Ph.D. from the University of Cambridge, where he taught machines to understand spoken English.

Use your brilliant brainpower to draw a single line that passes through every white square in the puzzles below. You can only use horizontal and vertical lines. The loop cannot cross over itself, or pass through any square more than once.

Here is an example solution to show you how it works:

a)

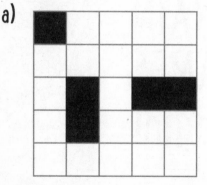

b)

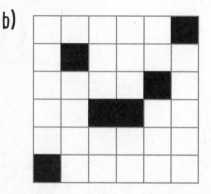

Whiz through this maze as quickly as you can, without making any wrong turns and getting stuck!

Start

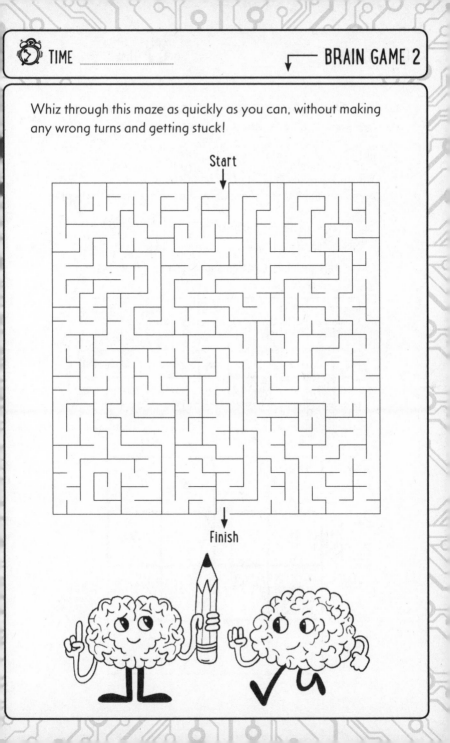

Finish

Can you fill in the empty squares so that the grid contains every number from 1 to 16 to create a number chain?

THE RULES

- You must be able to start at "1" and then move to "2," "3," "4," and so on, moving only to grid squares that are touching each other.

- You can move left, right, up, or down between squares, but not diagonally.

This example solution shows you how it works:

5		7		11
	1		9	
3		15		13
	17		23	
19		21		25

➡

5	6	7	10	11
4	1	8	9	12
3	2	15	14	13
18	17	16	23	24
19	20	21	22	25

	9	8	
11			2
16			3
	14	5	

Put your sudoku skills to the test and solve this puzzle. You must place a number from 1 to 4 in every empty box. You cannot use a number more than once per row, column, and marked 2 x 2 square.

This example solution shows you how it works:

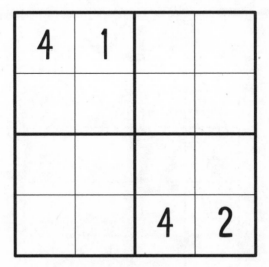

These clever brainiacs are giving you mathematical instructions to solve. Start with the number at the beginning of each chain, then follow each arrow in turn and do what the instructions say.

For example in the chain below, you would start with 15, then divide by 3, then multiply the result by 2, and so on until you reach the end of the chain.

Write your final answer in the empty box at the end of the chain.

To complete this brain buster, write either 0 or 1 in each empty square on the grid below so that there are an equal number of "0's" and "1's" in each row and column. You can't have more than two of each number next to each other in any row or column. For example, you could have 0, 0, 1, 1, 0, 1, but not 0, 0, 1, 1, 1, 0.

Here is an example to show you how it works:

0			0		1
0		1	1		
1			1	1	
	1	1			1
		1	1		0
1		0			0

→

0	1	0	0	1	1
0	0	1	1	0	1
1	0	0	1	1	0
0	1	1	0	0	1
1	0	1	1	0	0
1	1	0	0	1	0

0	0				
0				1	1
1	1		1		0
0		0		1	1
1	0				0
				1	0

To tackle this domino challenge, choose four of the spare dominoes from below to complete the domino loop. Dominoes can only touch each other if they have the same number of spots on the two touching ends.

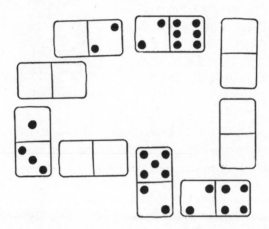

It's time for a cube contest! Can you count how many cubes there are in this 3D picture? This block of cubes started off as an arrangement of 4 x 3 x 4 cubes, like the picture below.

TOP TIP: Try counting each layer of cubes separately. For example, how many cubes are there on the bottom layer? Then add up the total number of cubes on each layer to get your total.

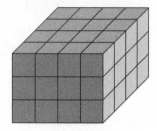

Some of the cubes have been removed, but none of the cubes are "floating" in the air, so if there is a cube on a layer above the bottom layer, you can be sure that all the cubes beneath it are still there too.

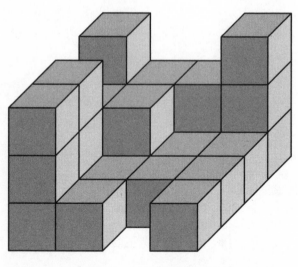

There are .... cubes.

Can you draw straight lines to join all of the dots into a single loop? You can only use straight horizontal or vertical lines, and the loop can't cross or touch itself. Parts of the loop have already been drawn in to get you started.

This example solution shows you how it works:

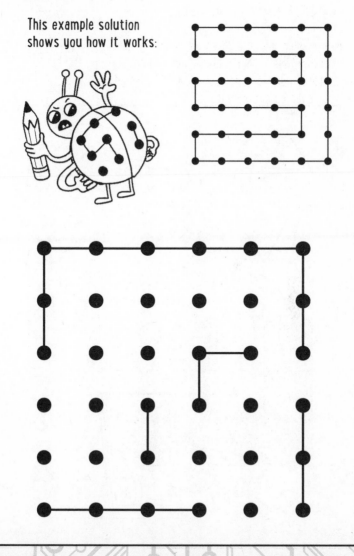

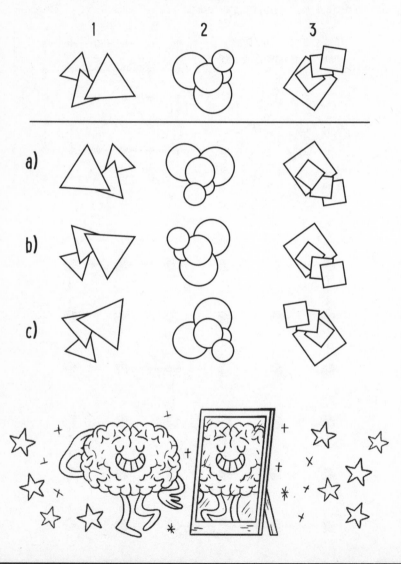

BRAIN GAME 10

🕑 TIME ....

It's time for a magic mirror challenge. Choose the correct mirror image reflections for pictures 1, 2, and 3 from the three options a, b, or c below and circle your answer.

1   2   3

a)

b)

c)

Both pictures below show the same background image, but in each picture different parts of it are covered by white squares.

Imagine the two images are combined to help you figure out these conundrums:

a) How many stars are there? ....

b) How many circles are there? ....

c) How many triangles are there? ....

Are you a total brainiac? Add together some of the numbers below to reach the totals at the bottom of the page. You can only use each number once for each total. For example, you could form 45 by adding 8 + 6 + 10 + 12 + 9.

Numbers:

8
6
10
12
7
9

Write your answers below:

a) 14 = ...

b) 20 = ...

c) 32 = ...

d) 38 = ...

Listen up! How many rectangles can you count in this giant rectangle? Include every one you can find, including the large one all around the edge. Don't forget that smaller rectangles can be combined to create one bigger rectangle.

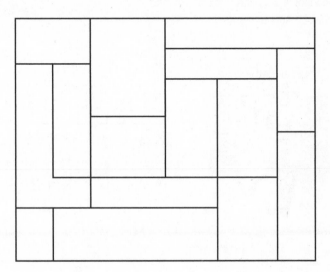

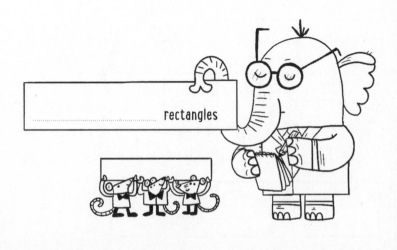

.... rectangles

⏰ TIME ....

Can you fill in each empty space on the pyramid to complete it? Every block must be equal to the sum of the numbers in the two blocks directly beneath it.

This example solution shows you how it works:

In the top three boxes, 52 + 59 = 111.

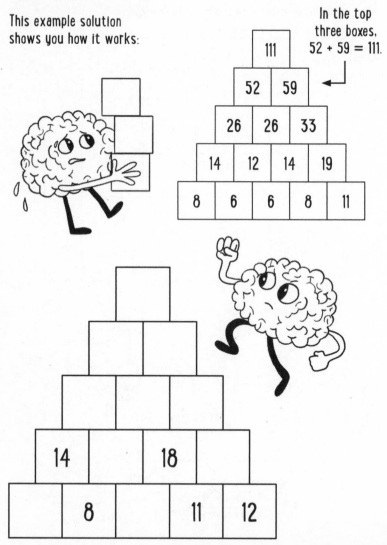

Hidden somewhere in the word net below is the word "CLEVER." Use your brainpower to find it! Start at one of the letter "C's" and connect the letters until you have spelled out the whole word. You can only travel along the connecting lines and you can't use the same letter more than once.

To see how it works, take a look at this solved example puzzle where "WORDS" has been spelled out:

Are you an alphabet aficionado? Place these words in alphabetical order to find out. Find a stopwatch and time yourself to see how long it takes you to alphabetize the words in Puzzle 1 and again in Puzzle 2. You might be surprised at how your times compare. Ready, set, alphabet!

Puzzle 1

Sausage   Burger   Ketchup   Bun   Salt   Vinegar

....

....

....

....

....

....

Puzzle 2

Three   Six   Two   Five   Four   One

How did your times compare? The words in Puzzle 2 are shorter and a little bit easier to spell, but did you find that you were slower? If not, congratulations! But most people are a bit slower, and the reason is that your brain "knows" that the "correct" order is One, Two, Three, Four, Five, and then Six, which makes it harder to concentrate on the alphabetical ordering.

Here are the six sides of a regular dice:

Unfortunately, some dots have gone missing from the dice below. Can you solve the questions below? The dice faces might be rotated compared to the example faces at the top of the page.

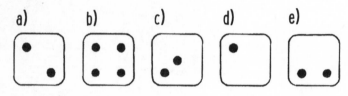

a) Which of the dice could be sixes?

b) Which of the dice could be threes?

c) What is the lowest possible total value of these five dice?

d) What is the highest possible total value of these five dice?

It's time for a picture memory challenge! Spend as long as you like studying the pictures below and try to remember as much as you can.

When you're ready, turn the page. You'll find some, but not all, of the same objects. Can you use your magnificent memory to figure out which ones are now missing?

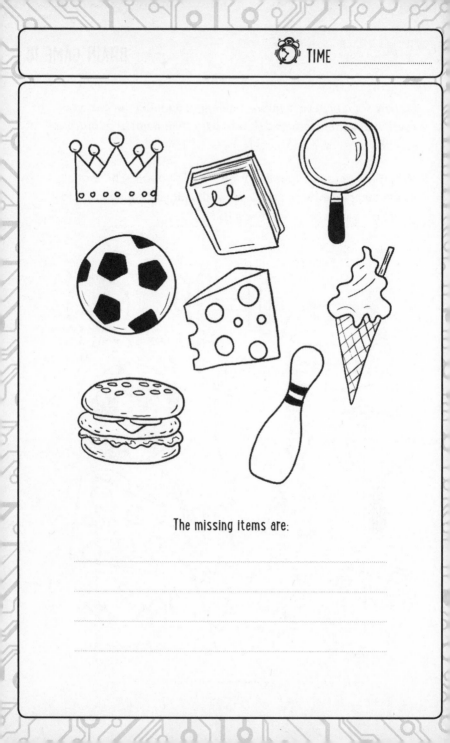

The missing items are:

....

....

....

....

Place a number from 1 to 5 in each empty square so that every number appears once in every row and column. Identical numbers can't be in diagonally touching squares.

This example solution shows you how it works:

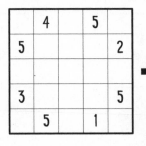

	4		5	
5				2
3				5
	5		1	

➡

1	4	2	5	3
5	3	1	4	2
4	2	5	3	1
3	1	4	2	5
2	5	3	1	4

	2	3	4	
	4		1	
1	2	3		

⏱ TIME ....

Can you figure out what comes next in each puzzle below?
Complete the sequence and draw the image in the empty box.

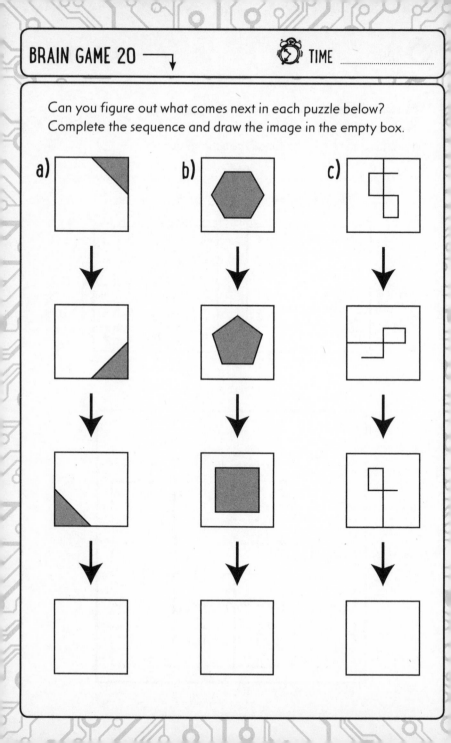

Use your brainpower to figure out which grid squares contain hidden mines.

THE RULES

- There can be a mine in any empty grid square, but not in any of the numbered squares.

- A number in a square tells you how many mines there are in the adjacent squares, including diagonally.

Take a look at this example solution to see how it works:

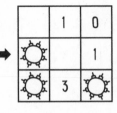

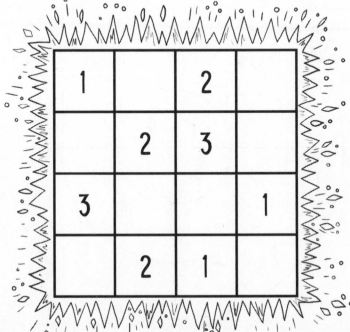

Can you form each of the totals below by adding together one number from each ring of this dartboard?

For example, you could make 12 by picking 6 from the innermost ring, 2 from the middle ring, and 4 from the outermost ring.

Totals:

a) 14 = ...

b) 28 = ...

c) 32 = ...

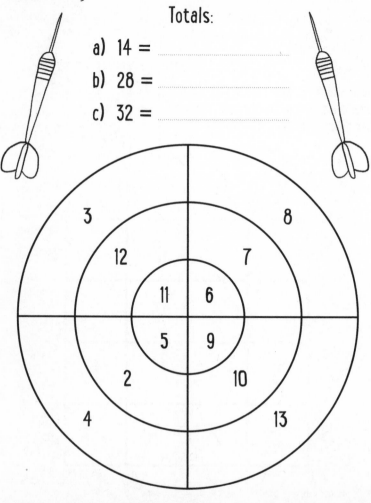

How quickly can you find your way through this extreme maze without getting in a muddle?

Time yourself and fill in how long it takes you.

The aim of this battleship game is to find a set of ships hidden in the grid. The ships vary in length, and there are multiple ships of the same length. Your task is to figure out which squares are just empty water and which contain part of a battleship.

THE RULES

- Each row and column has a number next to it indicating how many ship segments are in that row or column.

- Ships are always placed either horizontally or vertically.

- Ships don't touch each other in any direction, including diagonally.

Take a look at the example
below to see how it works:

1 × Cruiser
2 × Destroyers
2 × Submarines

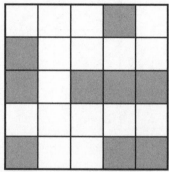

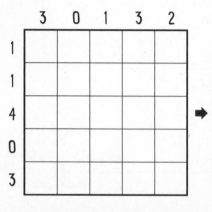

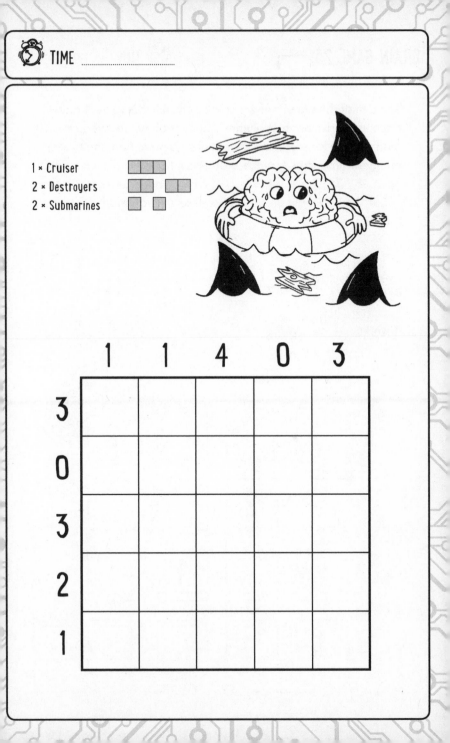

1 × Cruiser
2 × Destroyers
2 × Submarines

	1	1	4	0	3
3					
0					
3					
2					
1					

⏱ TIME ....

Solve this futoshiki puzzle by placing the numbers 1 to 4 once each in every row and column. You must obey the "greater than" signs. These are arrows that always point from the bigger number to the smaller number of a pair. For example, you could have "2 > 1," "3 > 1," or "4 > 1" since 2, 3, and 4 are greater than 1, but "1 > 2" would be wrong because 1 is not greater in value than 2.

Look at this solved puzzle to help you understand how it works:

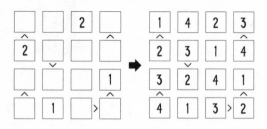

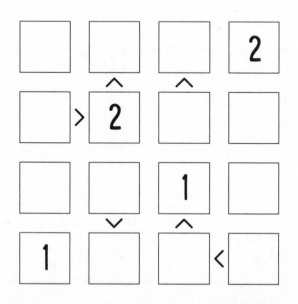

The names of some sports have been written down below, but each word has been broken into three parts and then all of the parts have been mixed together. Can you put all the parts back together to figure out what words are below? For example, TE + NN + IS would make TENNIS.

MIN	BAD	TBA
KET	FOO	TON
BAS	LL	BALL

....

....

....

Can you find ten sneaky differences between these two pictures?

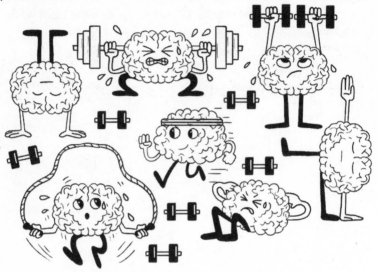

Get your brain in gear and figure out what number comes next in each of these mathematical sequences.

a) 11   14   17   20   23   26   ....

b) 51   46   41   36   31   26   ....

c) 2   4   8   16   32   64   ....

d) 91   81   72   64   57   51   ....

e) 17   19   23   29   31   37   ....

Can you build a word pyramid on the opposite page by solving the clues? When complete, each row will spell out a word that solves its corresponding clue.

Starting from the top and working down, each layer of the word pyramid uses the same letters as the layer above it, plus one extra—although they may be in a different order.

For example, if the first layer were CAT
then the second layer could be ACTS,
and the third layer could be CARTS.

1 C A T

2 A C T S

3 C A R T S

Clues:

1) A piece of wood cut from a tree trunk

2) A valuable precious metal

3) A rustic building that you might stay in on vacation

4) Yearned; really wanted

5) Sat down comfortably and relaxed

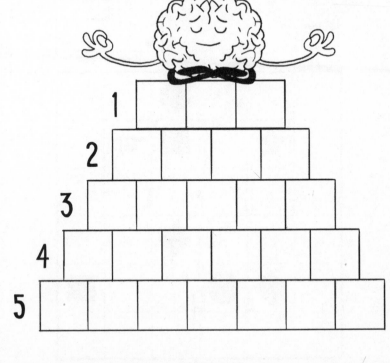

Super shape skills required! Can you draw paths to connect each pair of matching shapes together?

THE RULES

- The paths must not cross or touch each other.

- Only one path is allowed in each grid square.

- Each path must be made up of horizontal and vertical lines—diagonal lines aren't allowed!

This example solution shows you how to do it:

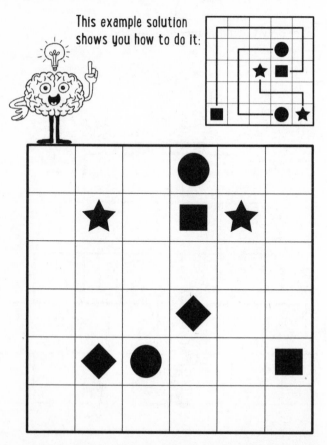

Can you solve it like Sherlock and find the matching image for the picture below? They might all look the same but only one is identical. Circle your answer below.

Complete the puzzle on the opposite page by drawing lines to represent bridges between the numbered "islands."

THE RULES

- You can only draw horizontal or vertical bridges, and each island must have the same number of bridges connected to it as the number printed inside the island.

- Bridges can't cross over either each other or an island.

- One line represents one bridge. There can be no more than one bridge directly joining any pair of islands.

- You must arrange the set of bridges so that someone could walk from one island to any other island, just by using the bridges that you've drawn.

This example solution shows you how it works:

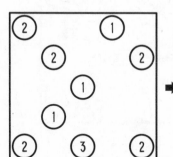
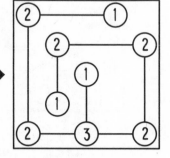

⏰ TIME ....

Something's not right here ... Use your powers of deduction to remove exactly one digit from each of the following incorrect equations so that they become correct.

For example, 12 + 3 = 4 would be correct if you deleted the "2" from the "12" so it reads: 1 + 3 = 4.

a) 5 x 12 + 9 = 14 ....

b) 10 + 20 + 30 + 40 = 90 ....

c) 23 + 34 + 45 = 82 ....

d) 91 + 19 + 28 + 82 = 200 ....

Can you solve this picture puzzle? It might look like these
pictures are all the same but there are actually four pairs of
identical images. Find the pairs and draw lines between them.

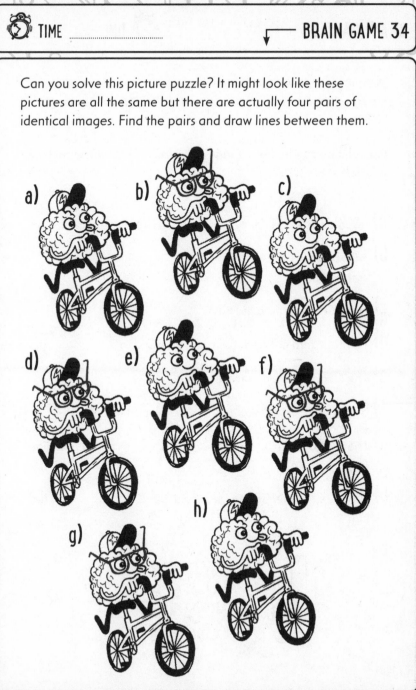

An anagram is a word that can be made by rearranging the letters of another word. For example, MILE is an anagram of LIME.

Can you complete these anagram puzzles? Don't forget to time yourself!

a) I would like to ADD my .... to the invitation.

b) All BETS are off as to the .... entry into the competition!

c) I was ABLE to sit on the hay ....

d) As the wizard entered the room, he BORE a ....

e) The CLERIC asked us to all sit in a ....

f) No CLOUD in the sky .... spoil this day.

g) The crowd RIOTED, or so the .... of the newspaper reported.

h) She used her FINGER to push back the .... of her hair.

The names of three animals have been mixed up in the letter soup cauldron below. Can you rearrange the letters to spell out the three animals? Every letter in the soup needs to be used, but can only be used once.

For example, you could use the B, A, and T to spell BAT. However, if you did that then you wouldn't be able to use the remaining letters to spell two more animals, so that's not one of the answers. Get mixing!

....

To solve these super jigsaw sudoku puzzles, complete the grid so that every row, column, and bold-lined jigsaw-shaped region contains all of the numbers from 1 to 4 once each.

a)

b)

Prepare to be brain-boggled! By drawing along the existing lines, can you divide this shape up into four identical pieces, with no unused parts left over? If you imagine cutting the shape into these four pieces, then each piece would have to be exactly the same once you rotated them all to point the same way. You can't turn any pieces over.

This example solution shows you how it works:

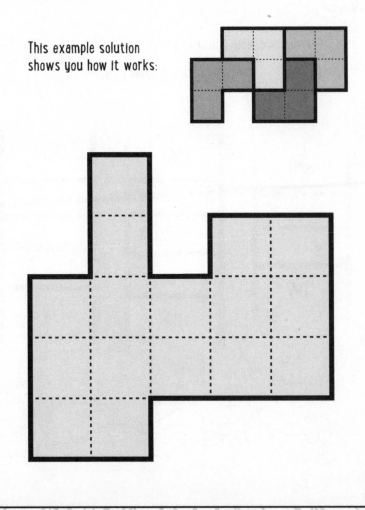

Use your incredible brainpower to climb these word ladders.
All you have to do is get from one end to the other, filling in the
gaps with new words.

Each word will have the same number of letters in the same order
as the word before it, but one letter will be changed to make a
new word.

For example, you could move from CAT to DOG like this:

CAT ➡ COT ➡ DOT ➡ DOG

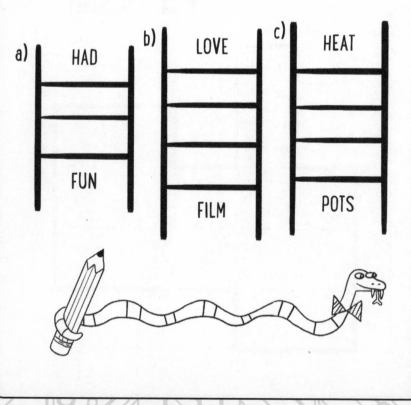

a) HAD

FUN

b) LOVE

FILM

c) HEAT

POTS

This field has four trees, four sheep, and four hay bales in it. Can you draw three perfectly straight lines on top of the field in order to divide it into four separate areas, so that each area has one sheep, one hay bale, and one tree?

Turn your brain upside down to complete this challenge. For each picture, 1 to 3, which of the options a to c shows its correct rotated version? The arrows indicate the direction of rotation. Circle your answers.

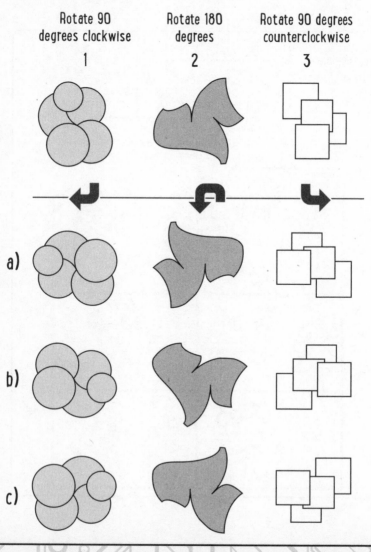

Rotate 90 degrees clockwise	Rotate 180 degrees	Rotate 90 degrees counterclockwise
1	2	3

To solve this sudoku puzzle, place a number from 1 to 6 in each empty square so that every row, column, and bold-lined 3 x 2 area contains every number from 1 to 6 exactly once each.

This example solution shows you how it works:

		1	4		
	4			3	
6					4
5					2
	5			4	
		3	6		

➡

3	6	1	4	2	5
2	4	5	1	3	6
6	3	2	5	1	4
5	1	4	3	6	2
1	5	6	2	4	3
4	2	3	6	5	1

2					3
		6	4		
	3			5	
	2			3	
		3	2		
1					5

Use this puzzle to train your brain to remember things!

A useful way to remember a list of things is to take the first letter of each word and then use those letters to make a new word.

Here is a shopping list for you to try to remember:

Meringue
Eggs
Mousse
Oatmeal
Rhubarb
Yogurt

The first letter of every word in this list spells MEMORY.

Now, read the list again, then cover it up and see if you can write down all six items below. Use MEMORY to help remind you of the first letters of each word. Ready, set, write!

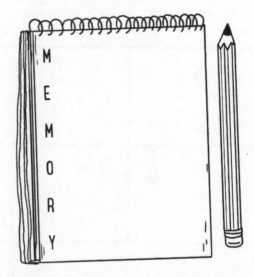

Can you conquer this cube conundrum? This cube started off as an arrangement of 5 x 4 x 4 cubes, like this:

TOP TIP: Try counting each layer of cubes separately. For example, how many cubes are there on the bottom layer? Then add up the total number of cubes on each layer to get your total.

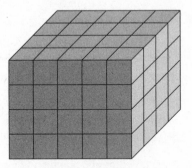

Some of the cubes have been removed, but can you count the remaining cubes and figure out how many are left? None of the cubes are "floating," so if you see a cube on the top layer, you can be sure that all the cubes beneath it are still there too.

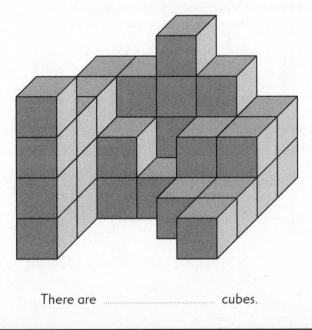

There are .... cubes.

Can you conquer the kakuro puzzle on the opposite page by writing a number from 1 to 9 in each white square?

THE RULES

- Place the numbers so that each continuous horizontal or vertical run of white squares adds up to the clue number shown in the shaded square to the left or top of that run.

- If a clue number appears above the diagonal line, it is the total of the run to its right. If it appears below the diagonal line, then it gives the total of the run directly below the clue.

- You can't repeat a number in any continuous run of white squares. For example, you could form a total of 4 with 1 + 3, but not with 2 + 2.

This example shows you how it works:

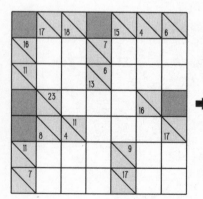

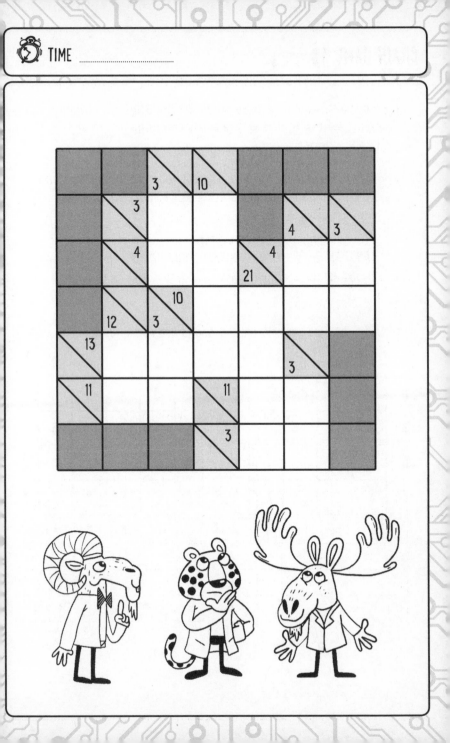

It's time to take on the astounding alphabet square challenge. Place the letters A, B, and C in every row and column on the grid on the opposite page.

The letters around the outside of the grid reveal the letter that should be in the nearest filled-in square in that row or column.

THE RULES

- There will be one empty square in every row and column.

- Only one of each letter can appear in each row and column.

This example solution shows you how it works:

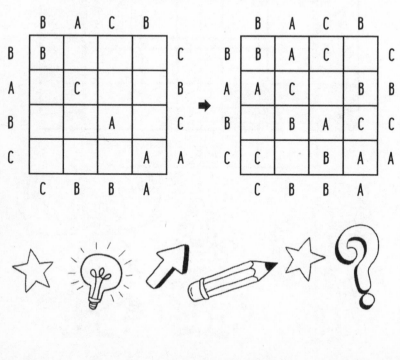

Are you ready for a hanjie challenge? Shade in the correct squares on the grid on the opposite page to reveal a hidden pattern.

THE RULES

- The numbers next to the rows and columns tell you how many squares you need to shade in.

- If there is just one number, then there is a length of that many shaded squares all together in the row or column—and the other squares will be empty.

- If there is more than one number, the first number of squares will be shaded, then there will be a gap and the second number of squares will be shaded.

This example solution shows you how it works:

For instance, there is 1 shaded square, followed by a gap of one or more empty squares, and then 2 more shaded squares.

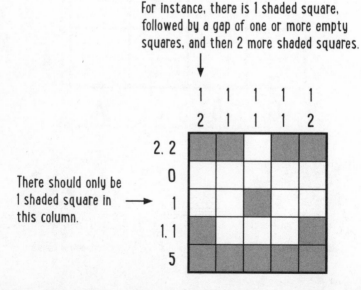

There should only be 1 shaded square in → this column.

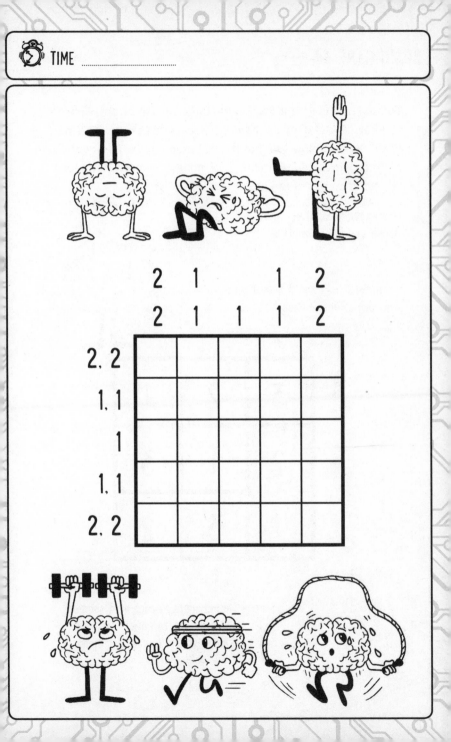

BRAIN GAME 48

To solve the calcudoku puzzle on the opposite page, place numbers 1 to 3 once each in every row and column. You must place these numbers so that the values in each bold-lined region of grid squares add up to the small number printed in the top left-hand corner of the region.

This example solution shows you how it works:

Numbers 1, 2, and 3 appear once in each column and each row.

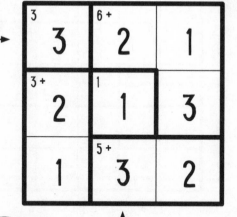

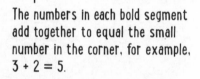

The numbers in each bold segment add together to equal the small number in the corner, for example, 3 + 2 = 5.

1	5 +	
5 +		3 +
4 +		

Picture magic! Can you use your imagination to figure out what this picture would be if all the pieces were put together correctly?

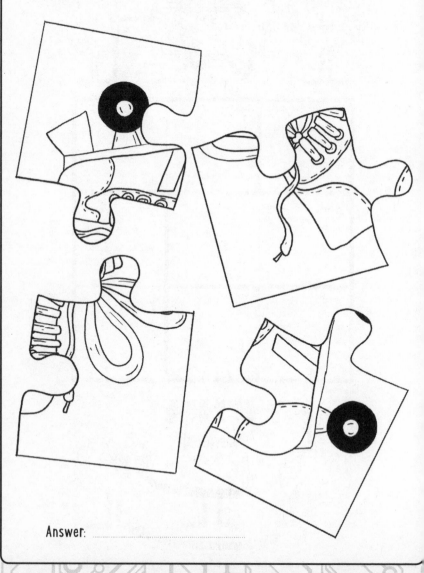

Answer: ....

Abigail, Brent, and Charlie all share the same birthday, and on their most recent birthday Abigail made the following observations:

- If you add my and Charlie's ages, you end up with Brent's age.

- In a year's time, Charlie will be half as old as Brent is now.

- A year ago, I was half the age Brent is now.

- The combined total of our ages is 24.

Can you use your logic power to figure out how old each child is?

Abigail is ....

Brent is ....

Charlie is ....

Can you solve these brain chains in your head, without writing anything down?

Start with the value at the beginning of each chain, then follow each arrow in turn and do what the math instructions say until you reach the empty box. Write your final answer in that box.

For example in the first chain you would start with 21, then divide by 3, then multiply the result by 7, and so on until you reach the bottom.

a)

b)

-3
+41
-17
÷2
10
START
×2

c) START

41
+31
-12
÷12
×2
÷5

⏱ TIME ....

Prepare for a brain teaser with this domino challenge. Draw along the dotted lines to create a full set of dominoes. There won't be any empty spaces left on the grid when you have completed it.

	0	1	2	3	4	5	6	
			X					0
							X	1
								2
						X		3
				X				4
								5
								6

Use this chart to cross off when you have added a domino. The dominoes that have already been added to the grid below have been crossed off on the chart.

5	0	6	1	2	5	4	0
1	2	3	1	1	3	3	5
2	2	6	6	2	3	6	4
4	0	0	4	4	6	5	1
3	6	0	6	0	2	5	5
4	1	3	5	2	4	6	0
2	1	0	4	3	1	3	5

TOP TIP: You can use the pieces that have already been placed in the grid to help you, as each domino piece is made up of two squares and the dominoes will completely fill the grid.

Use your brilliant brainpower to draw a single loop that passes through every white square. You can only use horizontal and vertical lines. The loop cannot cross over itself, or pass through any square more than once.

Here is an example solution to show you how it works:

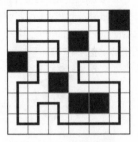

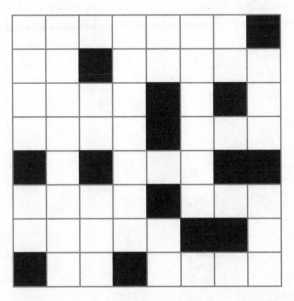

⏲ TIME ....

Draw horizontal and vertical lines to join pairs of circles, so that each pair contains one white circle and one shaded circle.

THE RULES

- Lines cannot cross over each other or cross over circles.

- Every circle must form part of one pair only.

Here is an example to show you how it works:

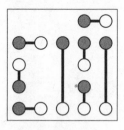

a)

b)

Can you complete this shape-shifting challenge and draw lines between each matching pair of shapes in the puzzles below?

THE RULES

- The paths must not cross or touch each other.

- Only one path is allowed in each grid square.

- Each path must be made up of horizontal and vertical lines— diagonals aren't allowed!

a)

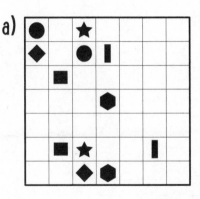

b)

You've woken up in a world where everything is triangular! Quick, get through this maze to escape the mayhem.

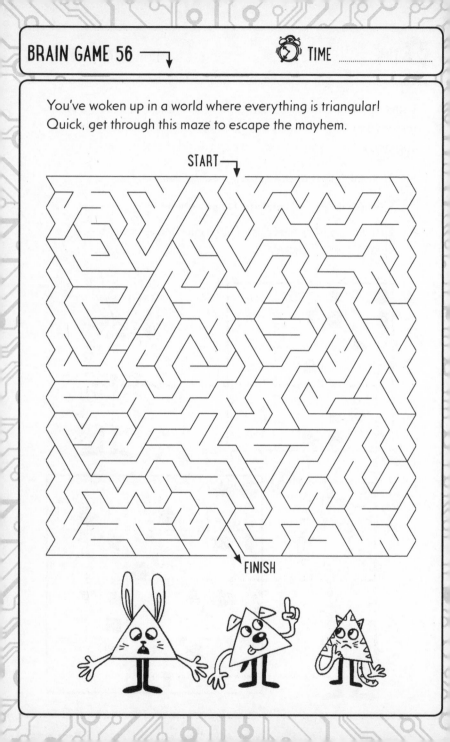

To solve this sudoku-X puzzle, complete the grid so that every row, column, marked diagonal, and bold-lined 3 x 2 region contains all of the numbers from 1 to 6 once each.

This example solution shows you how it works:

		3	1		
3	4	2	1		
6	1	3	5		
		5	6		

➡

6	1	2	4	3	5
4	5	3	1	6	2
5	3	4	2	1	6
2	6	1	3	5	4
1	4	5	6	2	3
3	2	6	5	4	1

	6	2	1	3	
	2			1	
	4			6	
	1	4	6	5	

⏰ TIME ....

Can you draw straight lines to join all of the dots into a single loop? You can only use straight horizontal or vertical lines, and the loop can't cross or touch itself. Parts of the loop have already been drawn in to get you started.

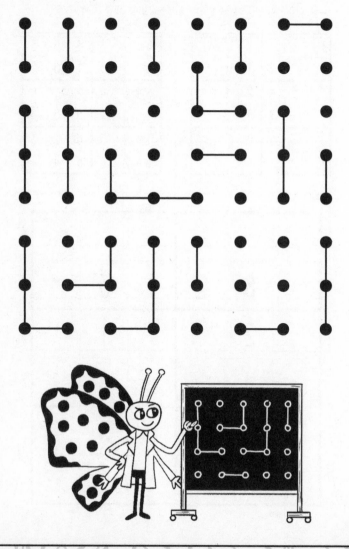

Write either 0 or 1 in each empty square on the grid below so that there are an equal number of "0's" and "1's" in each row and column. You can't have more than two of each number next to each other in any row or column. For example, you could have 0, 0, 1, 1, 0, 1, but not 0, 0, 1, 1, 1, 0.

0			0		1
0		1	1		
1			1	1	
	1	1			1
		1	1		0
1		0			0

🕐 TIME ....

Use the grid below to divide the white squares into different quadrominoes.

There are five types of quadrominoes, shown here:

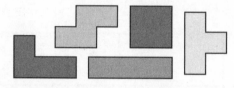

You might not need to use all five quadrominoes and you may need to use one type more than once. Don't leave any white spaces in the grid below.

THE RULES

- Don't use the black squares, they do not form part of any quadromino.

- Two quadrominoes of the same type can't touch, except diagonally.

This example solution shows you how it works:

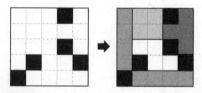

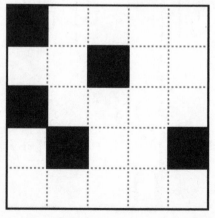

Place a number from 1 to 6 in each empty square so that every number appears once in every row and column. Identical numbers can't be in diagonally touching squares.

Here is a completed puzzle to show you how it works:

		2	3		
	4			5	
1					6
5					4
	1			6	
		6	1		

➡

6	5	2	3	4	1
3	4	1	6	5	2
1	2	5	4	3	6
5	6	3	2	1	4
2	1	4	5	6	3
4	3	6	1	2	5

1					5
		1	5		
	3			6	
	2			4	
		6	3		
3					6

The names of three numbers have been mixed up in the letter soup cauldron below. Can you rearrange the letters to spell out the three numbers? Every letter in the soup will be used once each.

For example, you could use the F, I, V, and E to spell FIVE. However, if you did that then you wouldn't be able to use the remaining letters to spell two more numbers, so that's not one of the answers. Get mixing!

....

Fill in each empty space on the pyramid to complete it. Every block must be equal to the sum of the numbers in the two blocks directly beneath it.

This example solution shows you how it works:

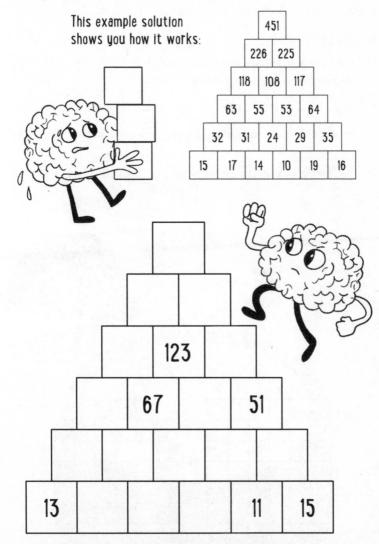

The aim of this battleship game is to find a set of ships hidden in the grid. The ships vary in length, and there are multiple ships of the same length. Your task is to figure out which squares are just empty water and which contain part of a battleship.

THE RULES

- Each row and column has a number next to it indicating how many ship segments are in that row or column.

- Ships are always placed either horizontally or vertically.

- Ships don't touch each other in any direction, including diagonally.

Take a look at the example below to see how it works:

1 × Battleship
1 × Cruiser
2 × Destroyers
3 × Submarines

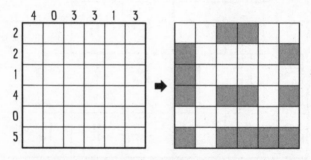

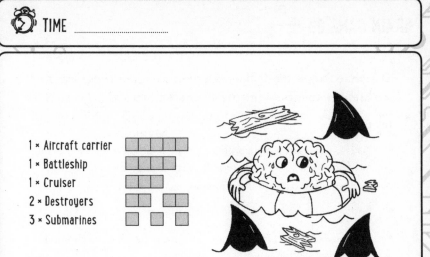

1 × Aircraft carrier
1 × Battleship
1 × Cruiser
2 × Destroyers
3 × Submarines

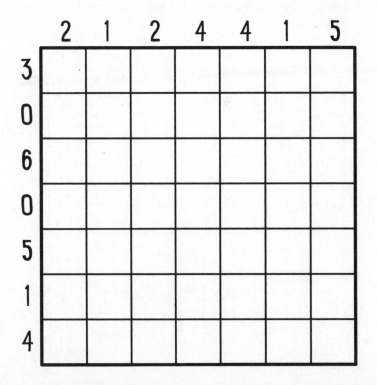

	2	1	2	4	4	1	5
3							
0							
6							
0							
5							
1							
4							

Complete the puzzle on the opposite page by drawing lines to represent bridges between the numbered "islands."

THE RULES

- You can only draw horizontal or vertical bridges, and each island must have the same number of bridges connected to it as the number printed inside the island.

- Bridges can't cross over either each other or an island.

- One line represents one bridge. There can be no more than one bridge directly joining any pair of islands.

- You must arrange the set of bridges so that someone could walk from one island to any other island, just by using the bridges that you've drawn.

This example solution shows you how it works:

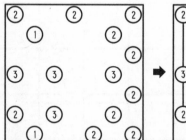
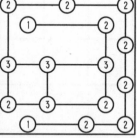

⏱ TIME ....

Fill in the grid below with white and gray circles so that you can travel from any circle of one color to a circle of the same color (gray or white) by moving left, right, up, or down.

THE RULES

- There cannot be any 2 x 2 (or larger) groups of circles of the same color.

- You cannot travel diagonally between colored circles.

Take a look at this solved example to see how it works:

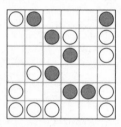 ➡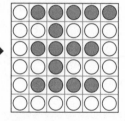

Boggle your brain with these number bricks. Place the numbers 1 to 5 once each in every row and column. Every 2 x 1 brick must contain one odd number and one even number.

This example solution shows you how it works:

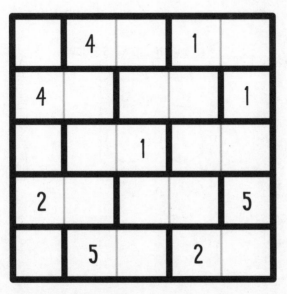

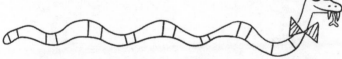

Challenge yourself with this mental arithmetic puzzle! Can you add together some of these numbers to create the totals below? You can only use each number once per total.

Numbers:

11
15
4
9
17
13
18

Write your answers below:

a) 20 = ...

b) 40 = ...

c) 60 = ...

d) 68 = ...

Listen up! How many rectangles can you count in this giant rectangle? Include every one you can find, including the large one all around the edge.

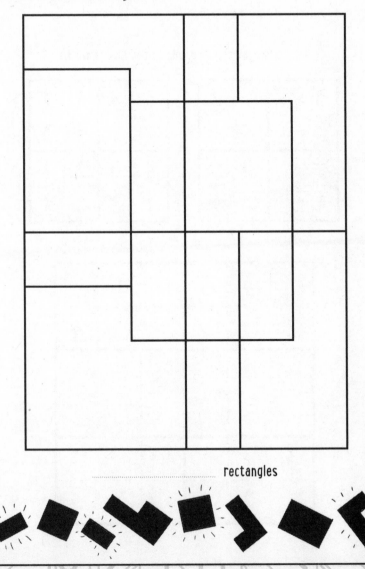

.... rectangles

TIME ....

Time for a super sudoku challenge. Complete the grid so that every row, column, and bold-lined area contains the numbers 1 to 6, once each. Even numbers must be placed in shaded squares and odd numbers must be placed in white squares.

Take a look at this example to see how it works:

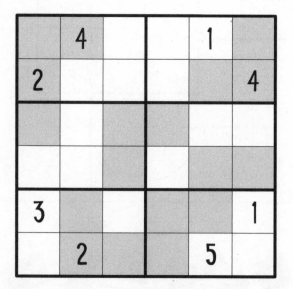

Can you form each of the totals below by adding together one number from each ring of this dartboard?

For example, you could make a total of 39 by picking 8 from the innermost ring, 10 from the middle ring, and 21 from the outermost ring.

Totals:

a) 30 = ...

b) 51 = ...

c) 52 = ...

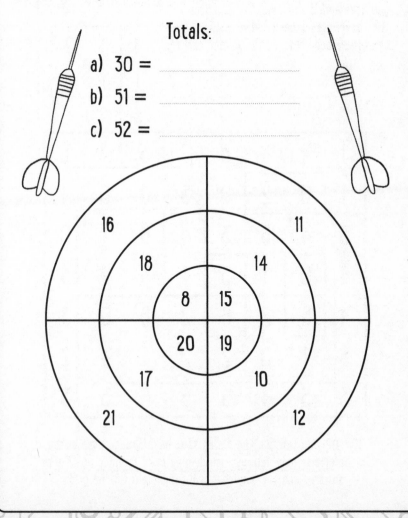

Prepare for a brain teaser with this domino challenge. Draw along the dotted lines to create a full set of dominoes. There won't be any empty spaces left on the grid when you have completed it.

Use this chart to cross off when you have added a domino. The dominoes that have already been added to the grid below have been crossed off on the chart.

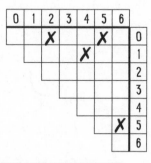

	0	1	2	3	4	5	6	
			X			X		0
				X				1
								2
								3
								4
						X		5
								6

1	4	6	6	2	3	1	5
1	0	2	0	5	0	0	4
3	4	6	3	4	6	1	0
4	0	1	5	1	6	2	3
4	5	2	6	2	6	0	3
3	1	0	2	2	1	4	2
3	5	4	5	5	6	3	5

TOP TIP: You can use the pieces that have already been placed in the grid to help you, as each domino piece is made up of two squares and the dominoes will completely fill the grid.

Can you spot ten subtle differences between these two pictures? You'll have to look quite carefully because the bottom picture has been reflected in a mirror for an extra challenge!

The following equation is incorrect, but can you move just one stick in order to correct it?

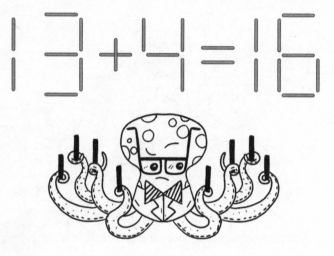

Now can you move two sticks in order to make this equation correct?

In the distant land of Farawaysia they have seven different values of coins, as shown below.

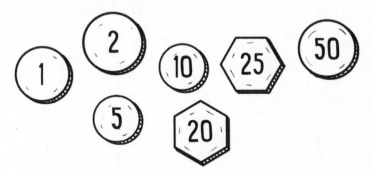

Use any of the coins you need to answer the following questions. You can use coins more than once if you need to.

a) What is the minimum number of coins you can use to spend a total of 73 Farawaysian pence?

....

b) If you use no more than two of any value of coin, what is the maximum number of coins you can use to spend 98 Farawaysian pence?

....

c) If I buy something that costs 149 Farawaysian pence, what is the minimum number of coins I could receive as change for 200 Farawaysian pence?

....

d) How many different ways are there of making up a total of 20 Farawaysian pence, without using more than two of any value of coin? For example, you could use two 10s.

....

There's a vowel thief on the loose! All of the vowels from these words have been stolen. Can you find the missing vowels to reveal the original words? For example, PLYFL would become PLAYFUL.

a) DRMNG ....

b) XMPLS ....

c) CLVRR ....

d) BRNST ....

e) WNNR ....

f) SSSSS ....

g) BLLNNG ....

Use your brainpower to unlock the answer to this tricky puzzle. Study the key below to figure out which imprint it matches. Only one is correct. Circle your answer.

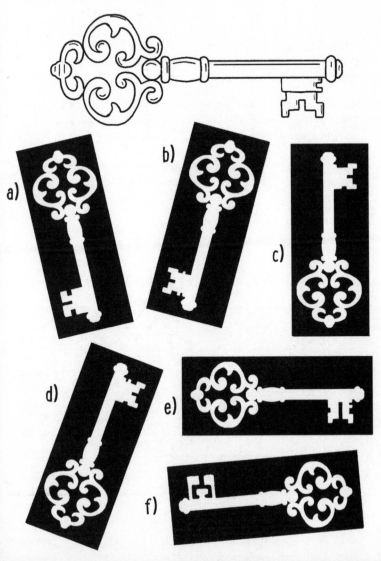

Can you conquer the kakuro puzzle on the opposite page by writing a number from 1 to 9 in each white square?

THE RULES

- Place the numbers so that each continuous horizontal or vertical run of white squares adds up to the clue number shown in the shaded square to the left or top of that run.

- If a clue number appears above the diagonal line, it is the total of the run to its right. If it appears below the diagonal line, then it gives the total of the run directly below the clue.

- You can't repeat a number in any continuous run of white squares. For example, you could form a total of 4 with 1 + 3, but not with 2 + 2.

This example solution shows you how it works:

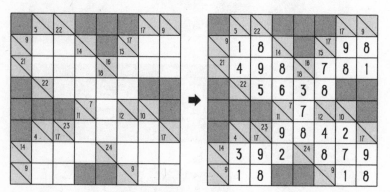

Can you crack these cunning codes?

1) You come across the following poster—can you figure out what it says?

PRES
SBEL
LTOE
NTER

2) Can you decode the following sentence?

Llew enod! Uoy evah daer siht!

3) And what about this next code? Can you make heads or tails of this?

Ere hne tti rws ieg ass emt erc esa

Are you a super sequence solver? Figure out which letter should come next in each of these sequences. Each sequence is a list of initials in an ordered set, for example, M T W T F S __ would represent Monday, Tuesday, Wednesday, Thursday, Friday, Saturday, so the next entry would be Sunday and the missing letter would be S.

a) O T T F F S ....

b) J F M A M J ....

c) H T Q F S S ....

d) R O Y G B I ....

e) M V E M J S ....

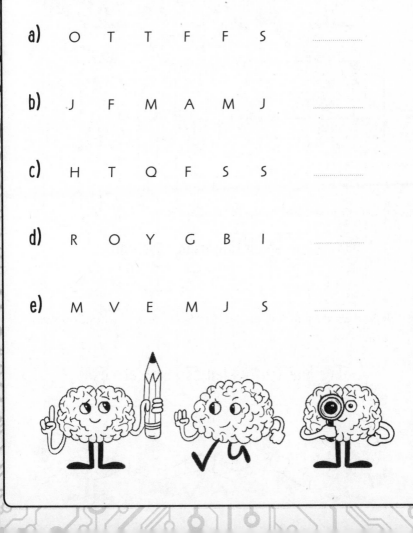

Make your way through this mind-bending maze as quickly as you can. You can go over or under the bridges as you wish, but beware of unexpected dead ends!

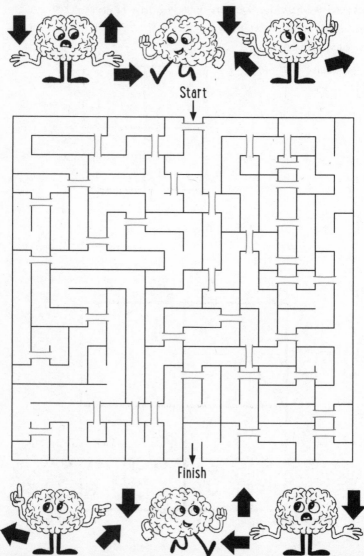

TIME ....

To solve this frame sudoku puzzle, place 1 to 4 once each in every row, column, and bold-lined 2 x 2 square, just like in regular sudoku. The numbers outside the grid tell you the sum of the two nearest numbers in the corresponding row or column.

This example solution shows you how it works:

2 + 3 = 5 ⟶

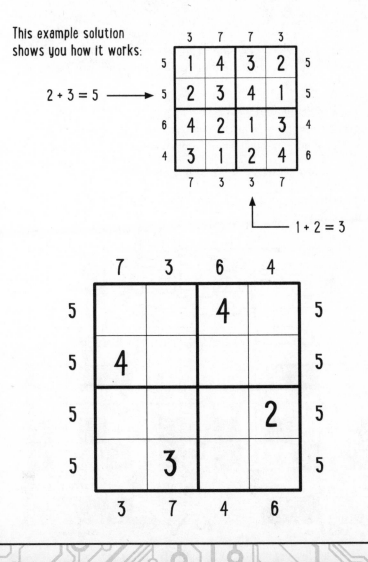

1 + 2 = 3

Use your lightning-speed brainpower to complete the grid on the opposite page. Every white square on the grid needs to be lit up by a lamp. A lamp will light squares to the left, right, above, and below it.

THE RULES

- Lamps shine along grid squares in the same row or column right up to the first black square they come across. They don't shine diagonally.

- Some of the shaded squares contain numbers. These tell you exactly how many of the touching squares (up, down, left, or right, but not diagonally) must contain lamps.

- A lamp isn't allowed to shine on any other lamp.

- You can place lamps on any empty square so long as the rules are followed.

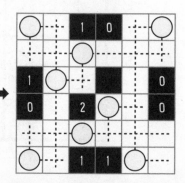

This example solution shows you how it works:

To solve the inequality sudoku puzzle on the opposite page, complete the grid so that every row, column, and bold-lined region contains the numbers 1 to 6, once each.

Inequality signs between some pairs of touching squares indicate that the number in one square is greater than the value in the other—the arrow always points to the lower of the two numbers. For example, "5 > 3," "5 > 2," and "5 > 1" are correct because 5 is greater than 3, 2, and 1, but "2 > 6" is incorrect because 2 is not greater than 6.

This example solution shows you how it works:

5 >		< 4 <			>
	>		3		>
		6			<
^			< 5 <		
	< 5				
			1		5

➡

5 >	3 <	4 <	6	2 >	1
6	2 >	1	3	5 >	4
2	5	6	4	1 <	3
4	1	3 <	5 <	6	2
1	4 <	5	2	3	6
3	6	2	1	4	5

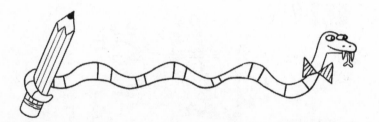

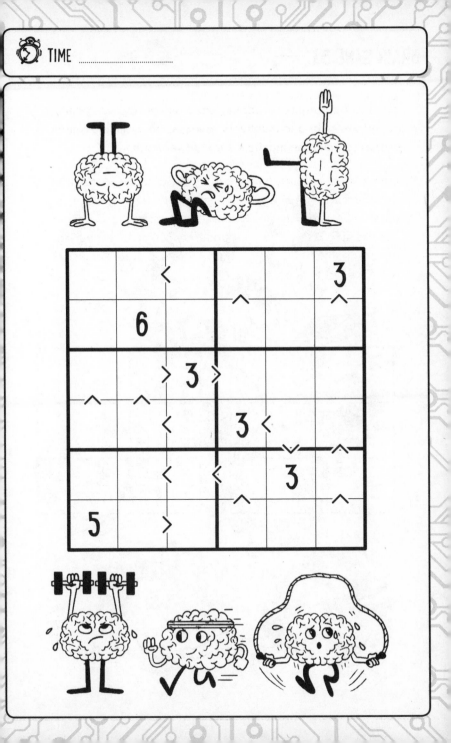

Where's the pair? These sneaky images might look very similar, but they are all hiding subtle differences. Can you find four pairs of identical images and draw lines between them?

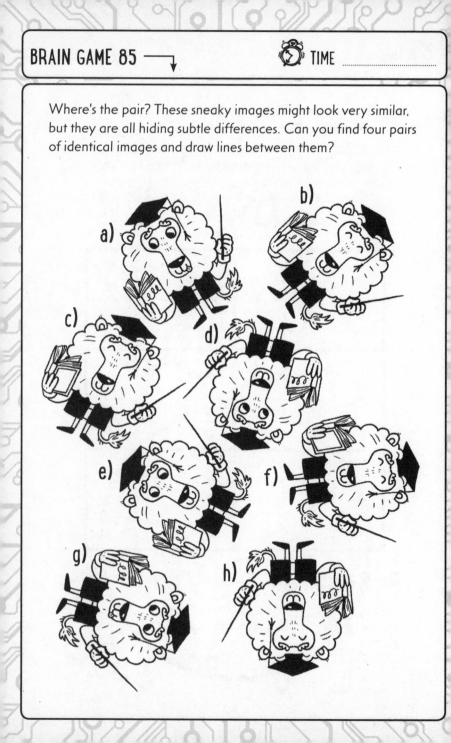

It's time for a dinnertime challenge. Before you're allowed to eat dessert, you must draw three perfectly straight lines on this dinner plate, to divide it into four separate areas. Each area must contain one French fry, one chicken nugget, and one pea.

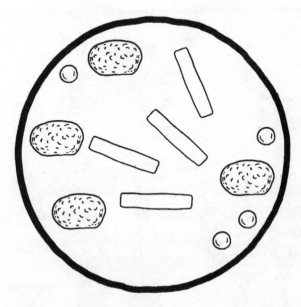

Five people have been arrested for a crime, and the police ask them to provide evidence about what happened. The five crooks each respond with a different claim, as follows:

Crook 1: Exactly one of us is lying.

Crook 2: Exactly two of us are lying.

Crook 3: Exactly three of us are lying.

Crook 4: Exactly four of us are lying.

Crook 5: All of us are lying.

Use your brainpower to figure out whether any of the crooks are telling the truth, and if so, who?

Answer: ....

Prepare to be brain-boggled! By drawing along the existing lines, can you divide this shape up into four identical pieces, with no unused parts left over? If you imagine cutting the shape up into these four pieces, then each piece would have to be exactly the same once you rotated them all to point the same way. You can't turn any pieces over.

This example solution shows you how it works:

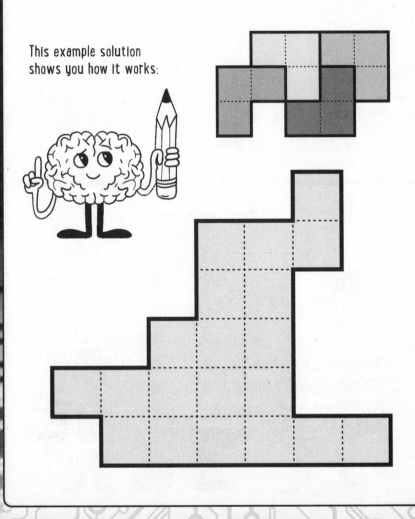

Solve this futoshiki puzzle by placing the numbers 1 to 5 once each into every row and column. You must obey the "greater than" signs. These are arrows that always point from the bigger number to the smaller number of a pair. For example, you could have "2 > 1," "3 > 1," and "4 > 1" since 2, 3, and 4 are greater than 1, but "1 > 2" would be wrong because 1 is not greater in value than 2.

This example solution shows you how it works:

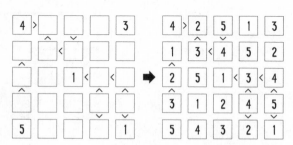

Can you solve this spooky silhouette challenge and find the matching image for the picture below? They might all look the same but only one is a perfect match.

Can you complete this mathematical grid? Place the numbers 1 to 9 once each in the nine empty squares so that each equation is correct. Calculate each sum from top to bottom or left to right, applying each operation in turn, starting at the beginning of each row or column.

Can you fill in the empty squares so that the grid contains every number from 1 to 36 to create a number chain?

THE RULES

- You must be able to start at "1" and then move to "2," "3," "4," and so on, moving only to grid squares that are touching each other.

- You can move left, right, up, or down between squares, but not diagonally.

Here is an example to show you how it works:

1				25
		22		
	12	13	14	
		10		
7				17

➡

1	2	23	24	25
4	3	22	21	20
5	12	13	14	19
6	11	10	15	18
7	8	9	16	17

7		9	12		14
1		35	36		18
2		34	33		19
26		24	23		21

⏱ TIME ....

Use your brainpower to figure out which grid squares contain hidden mines.

THE RULES

- There can be a mine in any empty grid square, but not in any of the numbered squares.

- A number in a square tells you how many mines there are in the adjacent squares, including diagonally.

This example solution shows you how it works:

	2	0		0
			1	
3		1		
	3		3	
		1		2

➡

✹	2	0		0
✹			1	
3	✹	1		✹
✹	3		3	✹
✹		1	✹	2

			3		1
	5	3			1
	3			4	
			2		
1		1		3	
	2		1		1

Picture magic! Can you use your imagination to figure out what this picture would be if all the pieces were put together correctly?

Answer: ....

To solve this calcudoku puzzle on the opposite page, place numbers 1 to 4 once each in every row and column. You must place these numbers so that the values in each bold-lined region of grid squares add up to the small number printed in the top left-hand corner of the region.

This example solution shows you how it works:

Numbers 1 to 4 appear once in each column and each row.

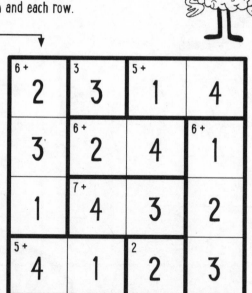

The numbers in each bold segment add together to equal the small number in the corner, for example, 4 + 1 = 5.

4 +	4	9 +	
	3 +	5 +	
9 +			4 +
		2	

Can you build a word pyramid by solving the clues? When complete, each row will spell out a word that solves its corresponding clue.

Starting from the top and working down, each layer of the word pyramid uses the same letters as the layer above it, plus one extra letter—although they may be in a different order.

This puzzle is really tricky, so don't worry if you can't complete it all! It might be a good one to discuss with an adult or a friend, so they can help you solve it.

For example, if the first layer were SOW
then the second layer could be ROWS,
and the third layer could be WORDS.

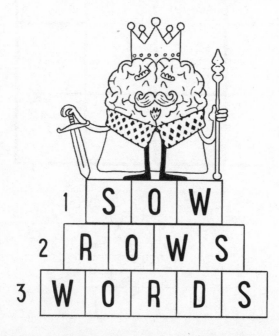

1 S O W

2 R O W S

3 W O R D S

THE CLUES

1) Something you write with

2) A type of evergreen tree

3) When fruit becomes ready to eat, it is said to _____

4) The son of a king or queen

5) A crab's sharp front claws

6) To plot against someone, for example, to overthrow a government

7) A senior police officer

8) The entrance areas of buildings

9) Impressions, as in your understanding of what is going on around you

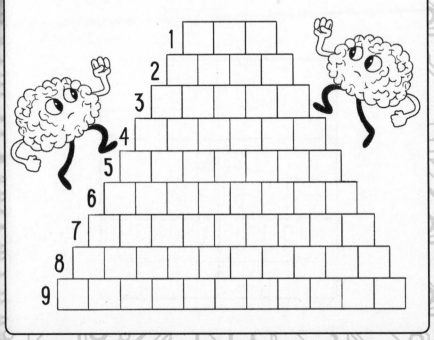

To solve this sudoku-XV puzzle, place numbers 1 to 6 once each in every row, column, and bold-lined 3 x 2 box, just like in regular sudoku.

Wherever an "X" or a "V" joins two squares, then the sum of those two squares is either 10 (for "X"), or 5 (for "V"), respectively—just like Roman numerals. If there is not an "X" or a "V" between two squares, then those two squares definitely don't add up to either 10 or 5.

This example solution shows you how it works:

4	5	3	6	1	2
2	1	6	3	5	4
3	2	4	1	6	5
1	6	5	2	4	3
6	4	2	5	3	1
5	3	1	4	2	6

6 + 4 = 10 ⟶

3 + 2 = 5

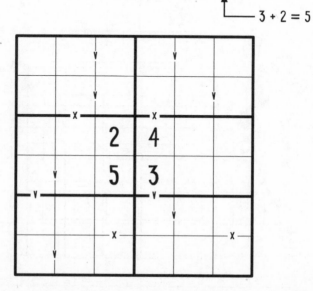

It's time to take on the astounding alphabet square challenge. Place the letters A, B, and C once each in every row and column.

The letters around the outside of the grid reveal the letter that should be in the nearest filled-in square, including diagonally.

There will be two empty squares in every row and column, and only one of each letter can appear in each row and column.

This example solution shows you how it works:

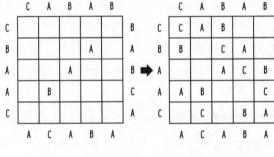

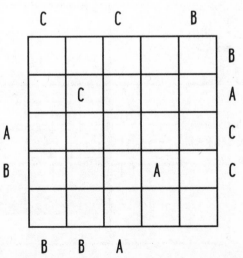

Are you ready for a hanjie challenge? Shade in the correct squares on the grid to reveal a hidden pattern.

THE RULES

- The numbers next to the rows and columns tell you how many squares you need to shade in.

- If there is just one number, then there is a length of that many shaded squares all together in the row or column—and the other squares will be empty.

- If there are multiple numbers, then there are as many sets of shaded squares as there are numbers, with each being of the length shown. They must also be placed in the order given.

This example solution shows you how it works:

For instance, there is 1 shaded square, followed by a gap of one or more empty squares, and then 2 more shaded squares.

There should only be 1 shaded square in this row.

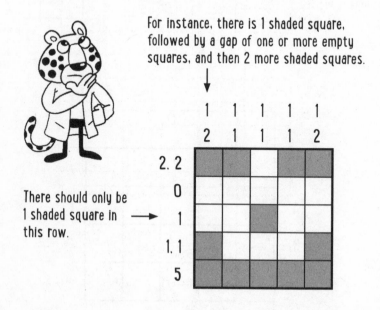

To solve this jigsaw sudoku puzzle, complete the grid so that every row, column, and bold-lined region contains all of the numbers from 1 to 5 once each.

This example solution shows you how it works:

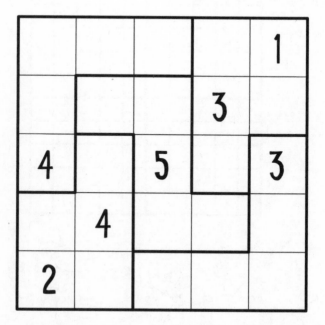

Isabella, Noah, and Olivia have each eaten a different piece of fruit at a different meal today. They had three meals—breakfast, lunch, and dinner, and three pieces of fruit: an apple, an orange, and a pear. Can you figure out who ate which piece of fruit, and at which meal they ate it?

THE FACTS

- Olivia had her fruit at a later mealtime than Isabella.

- Isabella didn't eat the pear.

- Noah didn't have his fruit for breakfast.

- The pear was not eaten for lunch.

- Olivia ate the orange.

Isabella ate ....

at ....

Olivia ate ....

at ....

Noah ate ....

at ....

All
of the
ANSWERS

BRAIN GAME 1

a)

b)

BRAIN GAME 2

Start

Finish

BRAIN GAME 3

10	9	8	1
11	12	7	2
16	13	6	3
15	14	5	4

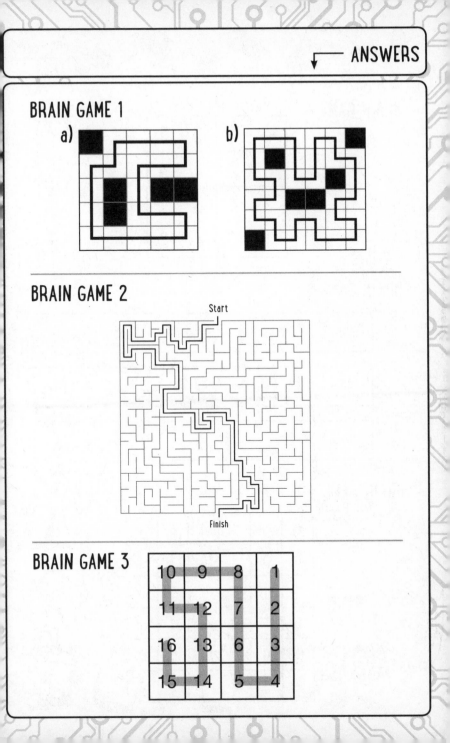

BRAIN GAME 4

4	1	2	3
3	2	1	4
2	4	3	1
1	3	4	2

BRAIN GAME 5

a)

15	5	10	70	53	59

b)

19	21	42	27	36	20

c)

18	27	9	26	13	52

BRAIN GAME 6

0	0	1	1	0	1
0	0	1	0	1	1
1	1	0	1	0	0
0	1	0	0	1	1
1	0	1	1	0	0
1	1	0	0	1	0

BRAIN GAME 7

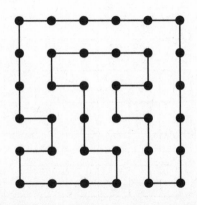

BRAIN GAME 8

27 cubes: 4 on the first layer (counting down from the top), 8 on the second layer, and 15 on the third layer.

BRAIN GAME 9

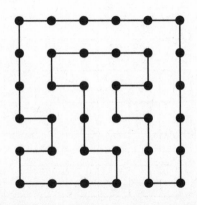

BRAIN GAME 10

1. b, 2. c, 3. b

BRAIN GAME 11

a) 5 stars   b) 7 circles   c) 3 triangles

BRAIN GAME 12

a) $14 = 6 + 8$

b) $20 = 8 + 12$

c) $32 = 6 + 7 + 9 + 10$

d) $38 = 7 + 9 + 10 + 12$

BRAIN GAME 13

There are **23 rectangles**.

BRAIN GAME 14

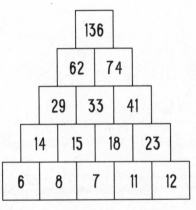

BRAIN GAME 15

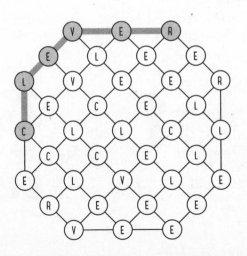

BRAIN GAME 16

Puzzle 1: Bun, Burger, Ketchup, Salt, Sausage, Vinegar

Puzzle 2: Five, Four, One, Six, Three, Two

BRAIN GAME 17

a) a, b, d, and e could be sixes.

b) a, c, and d could be threes.

c) The lowest total value is $2 + 4 + 3 + 2 + 4 = 15$.

d) The highest total value is $6 + 6 + 5 + 6 + 6 = 29$.

BRAIN GAME 18

The missing items are: **weight, lightbulb, flask**, and **domino**.

BRAIN GAME 19

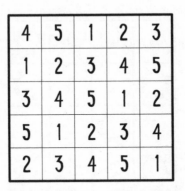

4	5	1	2	3
1	2	3	4	5
3	4	5	1	2
5	1	2	3	4
2	3	4	5	1

BRAIN GAME 20

a)   The shape rotates 90 degrees clockwise at each step.

b)   The number of sides on the polygon reduces by 1 at each step.

c)   The last line is deleted from the shape and the shape rotates 90 degrees counterclockwise at each step.

BRAIN GAME 21

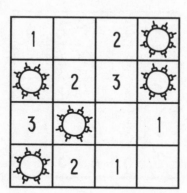

BRAIN GAME 22

a) $14 = 9 + 2 + 3$

b) $28 = 5 + 10 + 13$

c) $32 = 9 + 10 + 13$

BRAIN GAME 23

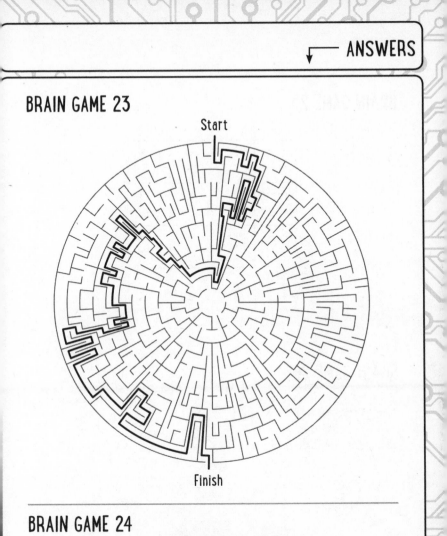

Start

Finish

BRAIN GAME 24

BRAIN GAME 25

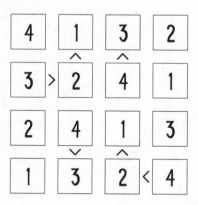

BRAIN GAME 26

The three words are:

badminton, football, and basketball.

BRAIN GAME 27

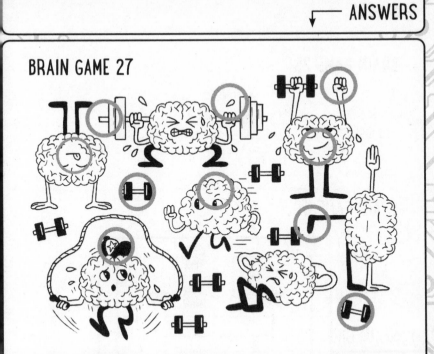

BRAIN GAME 28

a) 11 14 17 20 23 26 **29**
Add 3 at each step

b) 51 46 41 36 31 26 **21**
Subtract 5 at each step

c) 2 4 8 16 32 64 **128**
Multiply by 2 at each step

d) 91 81 72 64 57 51 **46**
Subtract 10, 9, 8, 7, etc. at each step

e) 17 19 23 29 31 37 **41**
Prime numbers in increasing order

BRAIN GAME 29

1. LOG
2. GOLD
3. LODGE

4. LONGED
5. LOUNGED

BRAIN GAME 30

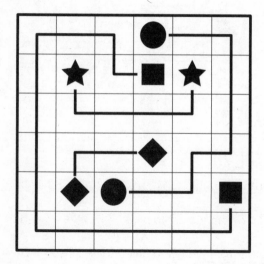

BRAIN GAME 31

The identical brain detective is **e**.

BRAIN GAME 32

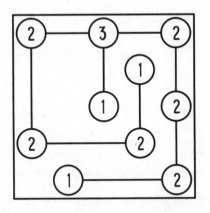

BRAIN GAME 33

a) **Delete the 2** from the 12 to give: $5 \times 1 + 9 = 14$

b) **Delete the 1** from the 10 to give: $0 + 20 + 30 + 40 = 90$

c) **Delete the 2** from the 23 to give: $3 + 34 + 45 = 82$

d) **Delete the 2** from the 28 to give: $91 + 19 + 8 + 82 = 200$

BRAIN GAME 34

The pairs of brains are:

a and h, b and d, c and e, and f and g.

BRAIN GAME 35

a) I would like to ADD my DAD to the invitation.

b) All BETS are off as to the BEST entry into the competition!

c) I was ABLE to sit on the hay BALE.

d) As the wizard entered the room, he BORE a ROBE.

e) The CLERIC asked us to all sit in a CIRCLE.

f) No CLOUD in the sky COULD spoil this day.

g) The crowd RIOTED, or so the EDITOR of the newspaper reported.

h) She used her FINGER to push back the FRINGE of her hair.

BRAIN GAME 36

The hidden words are:

dog, cat, and rabbit.

BRAIN GAME 37

a)

2	4	3	1
4	2	1	3
3	1	4	2
1	3	2	4

b)

3	2	4	1
4	1	3	2
2	3	1	4
1	4	2	3

BRAIN GAME 38

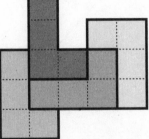

BRAIN GAME 39

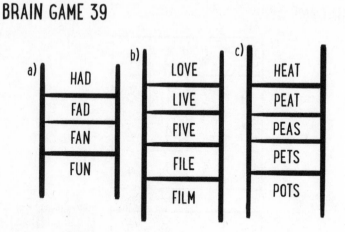

a)
HAD
FAD
FAN
FUN

b)
LOVE
LIVE
FIVE
FILE
FILM

c)
HEAT
PEAT
PEAS
PETS
POTS

BRAIN GAME 40

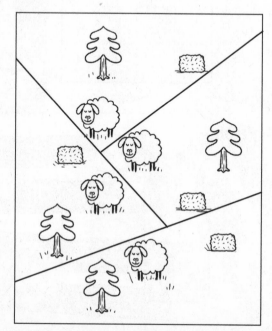

BRAIN GAME 41

1. c, 2. a, 3. b

BRAIN GAME 42

2	1	4	5	6	3
3	5	6	4	2	1
4	3	1	6	5	2
6	2	5	1	3	4
5	4	3	2	1	6
1	6	2	3	4	5

BRAIN GAME 44

35 cubes: 2 on the first layer (counting down from the top), 7 on the second layer, 11 on the third layer, and 15 on the fourth layer.

BRAIN GAME 45

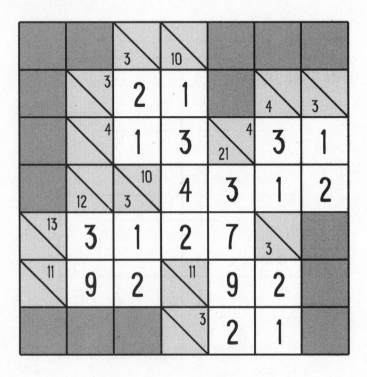

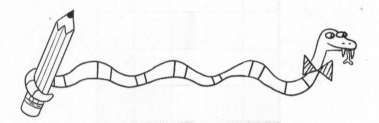

BRAIN GAME 46

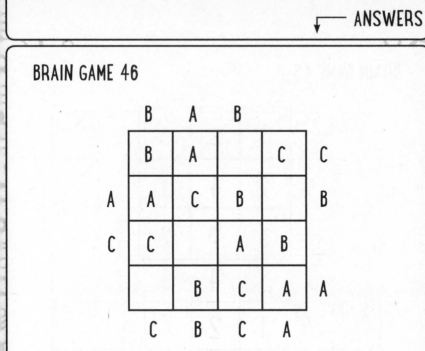

BRAIN GAME 47

BRAIN GAME 48

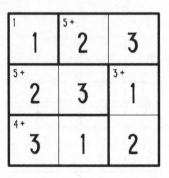

BRAIN GAME 49

A roller skate

BRAIN GAME 50

Abigail is **7**, Brent is **12**, and Charlie is **5**.

BRAIN GAME 51

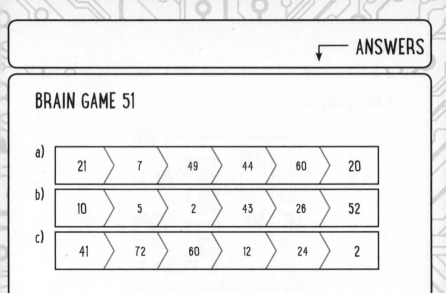

a)

| 21 | 7 | 49 | 44 | 60 | 20 |

b)

| 10 | 5 | 2 | 43 | 26 | 52 |

c)

| 41 | 72 | 60 | 12 | 24 | 2 |

BRAIN GAME 52

5	0	6	1	2	5	4	0
1	2	3	1	1	3	3	5
2	2	6	6	2	3	6	4
4	0	0	4	4	6	5	1
3	6	0	6	0	2	5	5
4	1	3	5	2	4	6	0
2	1	0	4	3	1	3	5

BRAIN GAME 53

BRAIN GAME 54

a)

b)

BRAIN GAME 55

a)

b)

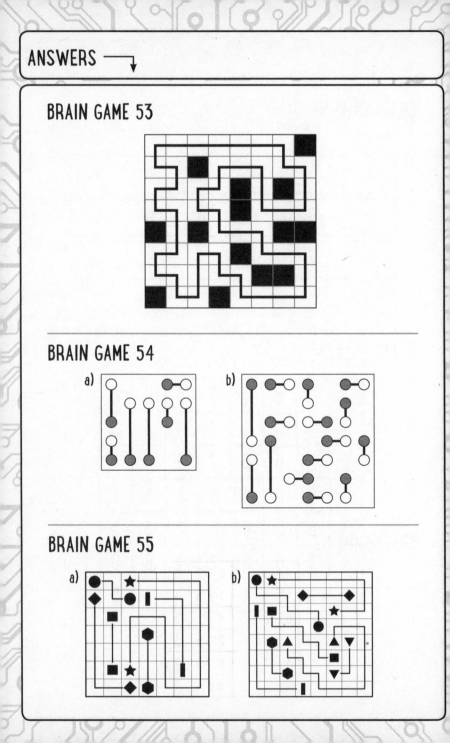

BRAIN GAME 56

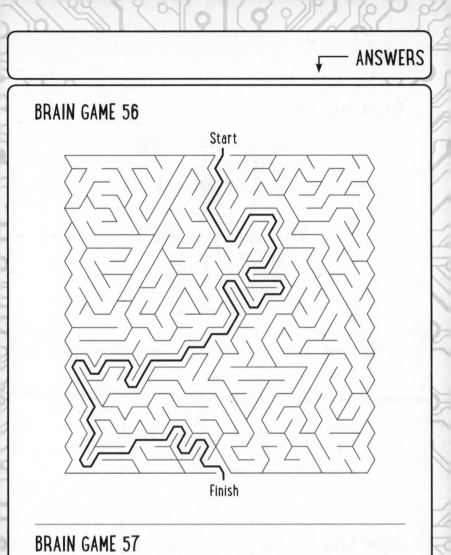

Start

Finish

BRAIN GAME 57

4	3	1	5	2	6
5	6	2	1	3	4
6	2	3	4	1	5
1	4	5	2	6	3
3	1	4	6	5	2
2	5	6	3	4	1

BRAIN GAME 58

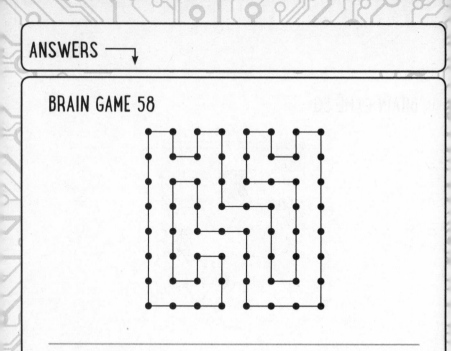

BRAIN GAME 59

0	1	0	0	1	1
0	0	1	1	0	1
1	0	0	1	1	0
0	1	1	0	0	1
1	0	1	1	0	0
1	1	0	0	1	0

BRAIN GAME 60

BRAIN GAME 61

1	4	3	6	2	5
2	6	1	5	3	4
5	3	4	2	6	1
6	2	5	1	4	3
4	1	6	3	5	2
3	5	2	4	1	6

BRAIN GAME 62

The hidden numbers are:

four, nine, and twelve.

BRAIN GAME 63

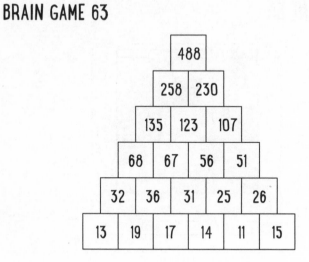

BRAIN GAME 64

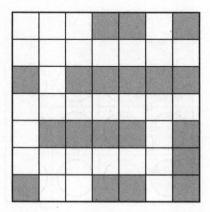

BRAIN GAME 65

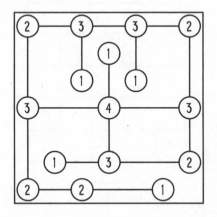

BRAIN GAME 66

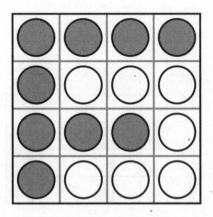

BRAIN GAME 67

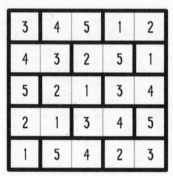

3	4	5	1	2
4	3	2	5	1
5	2	1	3	4
2	1	3	4	5
1	5	4	2	3

BRAIN GAME 68

a) $20 = 9 + 11$

b) $40 = 9 + 13 + 18$

c) $60 = 4 + 11 + 13 + 15 + 17$

d) $68 = 9 + 11 + 13 + 17 + 18$

BRAIN GAME 69

There are **29 rectangles**.

BRAIN GAME 70

6	4	3	5	1	2
2	5	1	3	6	4
4	1	6	2	3	5
5	3	2	1	4	6
3	6	5	4	2	1
1	2	4	6	5	3

BRAIN GAME 71

a) $30 = 8 + 10 + 12$

b) $51 = 20 + 10 + 21$

c) $52 = 19 + 17 + 16$

BRAIN GAME 72

1	4	6	6	2	3	1	5
1	0	2	0	5	0	0	4
3	4	6	3	4	6	1	0
4	0	1	5	1	6	2	3
4	5	2	6	2	6	0	3
3	1	0	2	2	1	4	2
3	5	4	5	5	6	3	5

BRAIN GAME 73

BRAIN GAME 74

$$12+4=16$$

$$20-3=17$$

BRAIN GAME 75

a) 4 coins: 50 + 20 + 2 + 1

b) 9 coins: 1 + 2 + 5 + 5 + 10 + 10 + 20 + 20 + 25

c) You would have change of 51 Farawaysian pence, so
   2 coins: 50 + 1

d) 4 ways:
   20
   10 + 10
   10 + 5 + 5
   10 + 5 + 2 + 2 + 1

BRAIN GAME 76

a) DRMNG = DREAMING

b) XMPLS = EXAMPLES

c) CLVRR = CLEVERER

d) BRNST = BRAINIEST

e) WNNR = WINNER

f) SSSSS = ASSESSES

g) BLLNNG = BALLOONING

BRAIN GAME 77

The correct key imprint is d.

BRAIN GAME 78

		10				19	16
	2	**2**	26	16	13	**4**	**9**
	17	**8**	**2**	**7**	9 / 26	**2**	**7**
	30 / 30	**7**	**9**	**8**	**6**		
	14	**6**	**8**	16 / 3	**9**	**7**	
	26 / 17	**8**	**9**	**2**	**7**	9	
17	**8**	**9**	11	**1**	**2**	**8**	
16	**9**	**7**			1	**1**	

BRAIN GAME 79

1) It says "**Press bell to enter**"—you should read left-to-right, top-to-bottom as usual, but the line breaks are in strange places and all the spaces have been removed.

2) Reverse the letters of each word to read "**Well done! You have read this!**"

3) Read the entire line backwards, and then ignore the spaces as given and insert some new spaces of your own. You will reveal "**A secret message is written here.**"

BRAIN GAME 80

a) S: one, two, three, four, five, six, **seven** (numbers)

b) J: January, February, March, April, May, June, **July** (months)

c) E: half, third, quarter, fifth, sixth, seventh, **eighth** (fractions getting smaller)

d) V: red, orange, yellow, green, blue, indigo, **violet** (colors of the rainbow in order)

e) U: Mercury, Venus, Earth, Mars, Jupiter, Saturn, **Uranus** (planets going outward from the sun)

BRAIN GAME 81

Start

Finish

BRAIN GAME 82

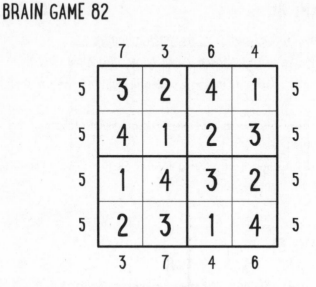

BRAIN GAME 83

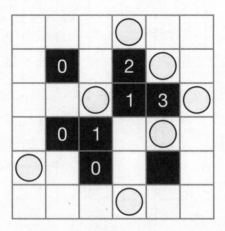

BRAIN GAME 84

4	2 < 5	1	6	3
3	6	1	4	2	5
1	4 > 3 > 2	5	6
2	5 < 6	3 < 4	1
6	1 < 4 < 5	3	2
5	3 > 2	6	1	4

BRAIN GAME 85

The pairs of lecturing lions are:

a and g, b and h, c and f, and d and e.

BRAIN GAME 86

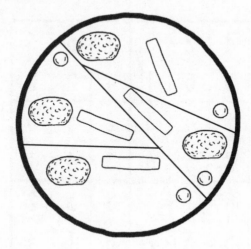

BRAIN GAME 87

If crook 1 were telling the truth then four of the answers would be true, but they are all different so this isn't possible. Similarly, if crook 2 or crook 3 were telling the truth then there would be two or more crooks telling the truth, which isn't possible for the same reason.

If crook 5 were telling the truth, then they would not be lying and they would have contradicted themselves, so they can't be telling the truth either. So we now know crooks 1, 2, 3, and 5 are definitely lying.

Crook 4, however, can't be lying, because if they were then we would now have all five crooks lying and we have already decided that crook 5's statement that all of them are lying can't be true. So crook 4 must be telling the truth.

BRAIN GAME 88

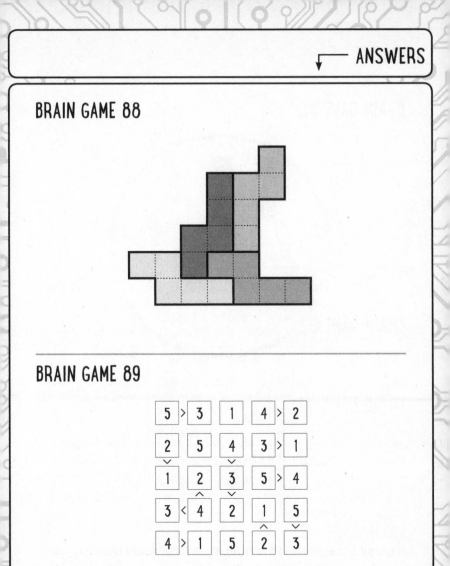

BRAIN GAME 89

5 > 3	1	4 > 2
2	5	4	3 > 1
1	2	3	5 > 4
3 < 4	2	1	5
4 > 1	5	2	3

BRAIN GAME 90

The correct spooky silhouette is C.

BRAIN GAME 91

3	+	1	+	2	=	6
×	■	×	■	+		
8	×	5	+	7	=	47
÷	■	×	■	−		
6	+	4	×	9	=	90
=		=		=		
4		20		0		

BRAIN GAME 92

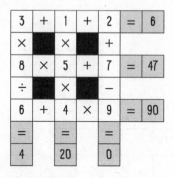

BRAIN GAME 93

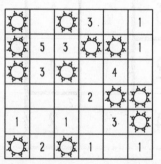

BRAIN GAME 94

A bike

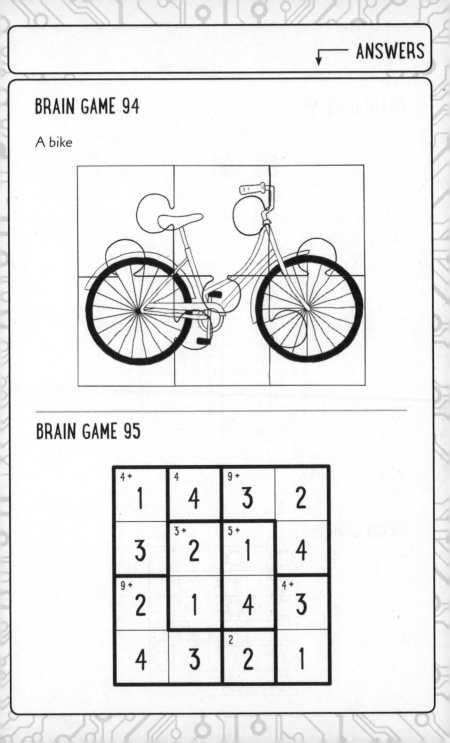

BRAIN GAME 95

4 + 1	4 4	9 + 3	2
3	3 + 2	5 + 1	4
9 + 2	1	4	4 + 3
4	3	2 2	1

BRAIN GAME 96

1. PEN
2. PINE
3. RIPEN

4. PRINCE
5. PINCERS
6. CONSPIRE

7. INSPECTOR
8. RECEPTIONS
9. PERCEPTIONS

BRAIN GAME 97

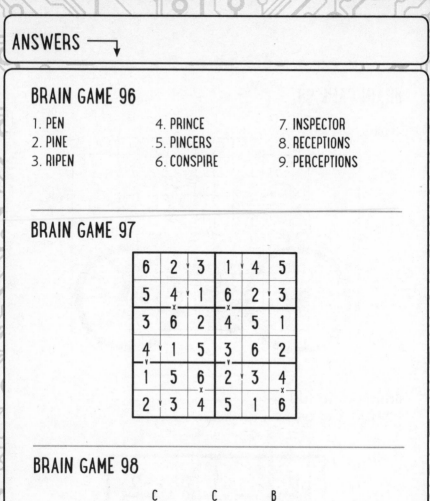

BRAIN GAME 98

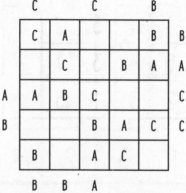

BRAIN GAME 99

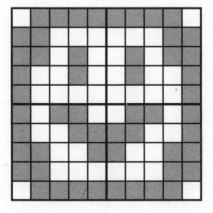

BRAIN GAME 100

3	5	2	4	1
1	2	4	3	5
4	1	5	2	3
5	4	3	1	2
2	3	1	5	4

BRAIN GAME 101

Isabella ate an apple at breakfast.

Olivia ate an orange at lunch.

Noah ate a pear at dinner.

You can solve this puzzle logically, without guessing, like this: Noah didn't eat his fruit at breakfast time, and because we know Olivia ate later than Isabella we know Olivia didn't have her fruit at breakfast either. This means Isabella must have been the one who ate fruit at breakfast.

We know that Isabella didn't eat the pear, and we're told that Olivia ate the orange, so Isabella must have had the apple. Therefore, we now know that Isabella had the apple for breakfast.

The pear wasn't eaten at lunchtime, so it must have been at dinnertime, given that we already know it wasn't breakfast. This means that Olivia, who we know ate the orange, had her fruit at lunchtime. The only person now left is Noah, so he must have had the pear at dinnertime.

The end!

Well done

NOTES
AND
SCRIBBLES